Delicate Tapestries

A Step by Step Guide to Raising
Eastern Black Swallowtail Butterflies

Photography and Text
by
Jill Marie Ocone

ISBN-13: 978-1463661571

ISBN-10: 1463661576

Published by PhotOcone...Photography by Jill Ocone

Contact the author at delicatetapestries@photocone.com

Table of Contents

"What the caterpillar calls
the end of the world,
the Master calls a butterfly."

- Richard Bach

Welcome to the world of the delicate tapestries that take flight each summer: the Eastern Black Swallowtail Butterfly. These beautiful creatures are very easy and inexpensive to raise. Ironically, I first started raising Eastern Black Swallowtail Butterflies completely by accident. In the late summer months of 2005, a friend gave me two curly parsley plants, and a few days later, I noticed two large green and black striped caterpillars on the plants. I searched the Internet and found out that the caterpillars were the larvae of the Eastern Black Swallowtail Butterfly. I am a high school English and journalism teacher with not much of an educational background in science, and was surprised that I could not find a book dedicated solely to the life cycle of the Eastern Black Swallowtail Butterfly. Thus began a quest of learning as much as I could about all four life stages of the Eastern Black Swallowtail Butterfly, as well as keeping a daily photo and written journal of what I learned and observed with each of the life stages during every summer since 2005. The result: "Delicate Tapestries," which is based upon personal experience.

Some people consider the caterpillar, also known as the "parsley worm," to be an invasive pest. In reality, most people grow parsley to use as an herb in their cooking and become irritated when their plants disappear. A container of parsley can be reduced to nothing when the caterpillars are in their later stage of life and do nothing more than eat, and eat, and eat.

However, I personally have found much enjoyment in observing the Eastern Black Swallowtail Butterfly circle of life. When I tell others about my hobby, which I kept a secret for a long time, most people find it to be rather interesting. In fact, I have had a few friends and students try to raise their own butterflies through my advice. I have also had friends and family members call me to come and rescue a caterpillar from their parsley, who then becomes a new member of my caterpillar family.

My hope is that after reading "Delicate Tapestries," you will be encouraged to raise your own Eastern Black Swallowtail Butterflies, thus adding more colorful beauty to our world.

Acknowledgements and Dedication

Just as I have been blessed with appreciation for each Delicate Tapestry that I encounter, I have been equally blessed with the encouragement of many special people, each of whom is a separate thread in my own life tapestry. I have the utmost appreciation and gratitude for the following people, whose support and belief in me kept me from giving in to self doubt: my fantastic husband Tony, my wonderful parents Barbara, Jim, Lou & Mary Lou, my fabulous brother Ross and my equally fabulous sister-in-law Hannah, my new nephew Harrison, my other terrific sister-in-laws Nicole and Maria, Uncle Glenn, Uncle Bob and Aunt Dolores, cousins Matt, Jill, Kerry, Bill, Aaron, Brielle and Lexi, my rheumatologist Dr. Arthur Brawer, and my friends Jennifer Gerics, Laura Kerwin, Jen Leeman, Erica Reinman, Noreen O'Donnell, Kristy Ansbach, the DeFelice family, Mandi Bean and Branden Kerr. Thank you to my Manchester Township High School family, who always shares my life journey through photographs and stories, especially Lisa Vecchione, Jane Williams, Abbe Clark, Gwen Koropatnick, Mary Ellen Hansen, Tracey Raimondo, Tara Gardner, Heather & Dan Staples, Carol Moroz, Cindy Singer, Danielle Fashauer, Sarah Steudler, Steve Fence, Shannon Taynor, Linda Saraceno, Linda Taylor, Stephanie Robertazzi, Jennifer Ansbach, Wes Moore, Brian Slota, Marjon Weber, Joe & Nancy Gawlik, Keith Eckert, John Musolf, Dawn Sullivan, Mo McCann, Brianna McKiernan, Vicki Trapp, Cathi Yayac, Mary Ellen DelNero, Val Schaefer, Lucy DiLeo, Erin Berhalter, Chrissy Velardi, Rene Ybarbo, Janeen Karaba, Dorothy Paul, Dorren Ferrone, Lauren Merolla, Alan Hammerschmidt, Sharon Boggs, Paul DeSilva, Ryan Ramsay, Todd Cornish, Mickey Williamson, Patricia Goley, Diane Higgins, Chrissy Wolfman, Annette Simone, Sweeney McKennan, Barbara & Dennis Smith, Ed Hudak, Craig Savitsky, Barbara Riley, Maryann Adams, Jeanine Colon, Joyce Dworkin, John Frizalone, Sarah Thiffault, Brenda Jernack, Joe Taylor, Ruth Caswell, Jim Kelly, Tim Apgar, Gerry O'Donnell, Sue Holland, Erica Martucci, Kim Farrell, Lynette Renda, Leah Rampone, Steve Ninivaggi, Carol Lyons, Trudy Hollis, Maureen Layton, Sue Wendel, Joan Bardenhagen, Joan Kamienski, MaryEllen Fecanin, Barry Sullivan, Shannon Findlow, Carolee Moore, Sara Pavao, Suzanne DiFiore, Janet Ginda, Alex George, Evelyn Swift, Keith Lister, Connie Soper, Kevin Burger, Meghan Rabenstein, Dan Keiser, and David Trethaway. To all of my former students, thank you for your inspiration, especially Brian and Vali, who assisted with editing. Extra special thanks to my niece Emily and my nephew Nicholas, who often join me in the search for nature's creatures and allow me to see our world through their eyes.

"Delicate Tapestries" is dedicated to the memory of my brother-in-law, Michael Ocone (the businessman), my friend, Pete Giovenco (the artist), and my former students, Corporal Nicholas Ott and Sergeant Ronald A. Kubik (the heroes).

My life tapestry would be less colorful had these four outstanding gentlemen not left their permanent footprints and everlasting inspiration along my journey.

6

The number one item you will need if you want to raise Eastern Black Swallowtail Butterflies is bait. Make sure you have some parsley plants outside in your yard. I find that curly parsley works as the best bait, as I have had more eggs laid on curly parsley than flat/Italian parsley. You can fill a nice garden container with your parsley plants. More than one plant, especially in more than one area, will yield more eggs. Rather than growing the parsley from seed, I buy plants from a local nursery, and my parsley containers are planted by mid May. Dill and fennel are also host plants for the Eastern Black Swallowtail Butterfly and caterpillar, but since I have only used parsley, that is the plant I will focus on throughout the book.

In preparation for the upcoming butterfly season, by the end of May, I always have my materials ready to go. These are the other materials that I use each year:

• A "nursery." I use an old fishtank with a screen cover, and I keep it in the shade under a table, protecting it from rainstorms and direct sunlight. You can also use a clear plastic storage bin with a mesh cover. Even if you keep the nursery under a table, rainwater can still accumulate during bad storms. Keep your nursery as dry as possible and remove any standing water as soon as you notice it in order to prevent your caterpillars and butterflies from drowning. Never use a solid cover on your nursery, which can subject your caterpillars, chrysalises and butterflies to excessive heat or suffocation, resulting in their untimely death.

• Empty plastic containers and lids, such as the type of containers that soup or deli salads come in. Poke holes in the lids to insert cut parsley, but make sure the holes are only as big as the thickness of parsley stems. Caterpillars may crawl through holes that are too big, which can result in drowning or starvation. Have a few extra clean containers and lids on hand, which will make it easier for you to replace parsley in the future.

• Feeder parsley. While homegrown parsley is best, store bought parsley works just as well but rinse it thoroughly with water to remove all potentially harmful pesticides and chemicals. Otherwise, your caterpillars may die (which I learned, unfortunately, from personal experience). Once you have a caterpillar, fill the container with water almost to the top, put the lid back on, trim feeder parsley stems as needed, and insert the parsley stems into the holes, one stem at a time. If a hole is too big, put more than one parsley stem into it. Always make sure your parsley is fresh, and replace eaten or old parsley with fresh parsley containers as often as needed by placing next to the old parsley. Eventually, your caterpillars will crawl onto the new parsley and then you can remove the old container.

• Sticks. Those which routinely fall from trees are fine to use. Sticks must be clean and pest-free with no leaves. Arrange them in your nursery around the parsley containers at various heights once your caterpillars are at least a week old.

• Daily Care. Clean your nursery regularly to avoid bacteria and mold (see Page 13). During the summer heat, frequently check your parsley containers for any kind of algae buildup, which is not uncommon but should be cleaned as soon as possible. When replacing parsley containers, wash and completely rinse them to remove all soap, old parsley remnants, droppings and dirt.

• Camera and notebook. You might want to keep a photo or written journal to chronicle what you observe each day on the journey you share with your delicate tapestries.

The typical turn-around time from egg to butterfly is about 30 days in the summer months.

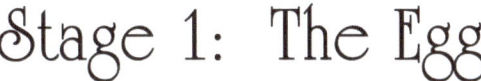

The egg of the Eastern Black Swallowtail Butterfly is pale yellow, round, and about the size of a pin head. Eggs are usually laid in the morning or early afternoon hours. Female butterflies will lay eggs on both the tops and the bottoms of parsley leaves. Later in the season, female butterflies will also lay eggs on flowering parsley stems and flowers. From my experience, female butterflies lay more eggs on curly parsley versus flat/Italian parsley.

Where I live in New Jersey, eggs begin to appear as early as the third week of May, and female butterflies will stop laying eggs sometime in early September. If you see an Eastern Black Swallowtail Butterfly in your area, then it is time to regularly check your parsley for eggs.

When first laid, the egg is pale yellow, and over the next few days, it will darken in color.

About 3 to 4 days after being first laid, the egg will turn either black or clear. When an egg turns black, a caterpillar is forming inside it and will most likely emerge soon. It can be a few hours, or even a few days, for him to come out of his egg.

Clear eggs will not produce a caterpillar.

Eastern Black Swallowtail egg, 1 day old

Notice how little the eggs are, in comparison to a human finger.

Above Left: A newly laid egg, approximately two hours old, is very pale yellow in color.
Above Right: This egg is one day old and its color has darkened to a deeper yellow.

This 4 day old egg has turned black because the caterpillar is forming inside it.

Left Photo:

When the egg turns black, the caterpillar should emerge soon.

Right Photo:

A clear egg will not produce a caterpillar.

When it is time, the caterpillar will rapidly emerge from his egg, within seconds. Immediately after hatching, the caterpillar will eat his egg. He will be about the size of a grain of rice, and will be light brown in color. Within an hour, the caterpillar's color will darken, and he will most likely wander away from the area where his egg was. The caterpillar will stay this size for about 24 hours.

Above Photos:

The caterpillar, newly hatched and minutes old, eats his egg. A newer egg near him is not ready to hatch.

Right Photo:

A different caterpillar, only a day old, begins to roam around the parsley. The egg on the underside of the parsley leaf to the left has a dark ring of color around it. The dark ring indicates that a caterpillar is beginning to form inside the egg.

After a new caterpillar emerges from his egg on your bait, carefully cut off the leaf he is on and transfer it to your nursery. You can simply lay the leaf on top of parsley leaves already waiting in your nursery containers. He will eventually crawl off the loose leaf, and once he roams off the leaf, remove it from the nursery.

You will be taking some risks if you do not transfer newly hatched or young caterpillars from the bait plant to the nursery. First of all, your bait parsley will most likely disappear, because the caterpillar will eventually eat most, if not, all of it. Also, the caterpillar will be exposed to predators such as spiders and birds, which will turn him into a tasty meal.

Nature knows best, and there are times when black eggs will not hatch. Don't get upset if your egg doesn't hatch or turns clear. Just gently remove the clear or unhatched eggs after you are certain that they will not produce a caterpillar. It simply wasn't meant to be for such eggs.

The caterpillar, or larva, stage lasts anywhere from 9 to 18 days. Caterpillars will "molt," or shed their skin, up to five times during this stage of their lives. The stages between the molts are called "instars." Watch your caterpillar on a daily basis, because every day he will grow bigger. What started out about the size of a grain of rice will eventually grow to be the length and width of an average human pinky finger.

Preparing the Nursery: Before introducing a caterpillar to your nursery, make sure you have followed all of the instructions in the "Materials You Will Need" section on Pages 7 and 8, and that your nursery is clean and ready to go with plenty of fresh and well-rinsed feeder parsley available. You may want to triple check to make sure that your nursery is not in direct sunlight or in an area which might inadvertently lead to rainwater buildup inside it.

Each of the caterpillars shown here are all one day old and in the first instar stage. While in the first instar stage, they turn darker in color and their white stripe becomes more defined each day.

<u>Now What?</u> A caterpillar's main jobs are to eat and to poop. Once you have put a caterpillar into the nursery, make sure he has plenty of fresh parsley to munch on. As he grows, so will the amount of parsley he eats on a daily basis. Caterpillar poop is called "frass," and the more he eats, the more frass will appear in the nursery. It is a good idea to clean out your nursery regularly to avoid mold and bacteria. Simply remove the parsley containers and rinse out the nursery with a garden hose or use a mild detergent, but thoroughly rinse any soapy residue. You can also cover the bottom of the nursery with paper towels, newspaper or wax paper to make the frass removal easier.

<u>Oh No! Is he dead?</u> In the event that a caterpillar appears to have drowned in either parsley containers or from rainwater buildup, don't lose hope right away. Believe it or not, an apparently drowned caterpillar can, somehow, revive himself. Just put him on top of an area of parsley after carefully drying him off with a paper towel and periodically check on him. Once I had a caterpillar come back to life about a day after I thought he had drowned. However, if the caterpillar does not move after a few days, my best guess would be to remove him and to give him a proper burial. Unfortunately, some caterpillars do not make it, and if you have a caterpillar that dies, remove him from the nursery when you are certain he has passed on.

*Top Left: Caterpillar 3 days old,
second instar stage
Top Right: Caterpillar 5 days old,
third instar stage
Bottom Left: Caterpillar 11 days old,
fifth instar stage*

The Caterpillar's Defense Mechanism

No matter how old he is, a caterpillar will use his defense mechanism when he feels threatened or becomes agitated or afraid. This may happen when you are introducing a new caterpillar to the nursery, or when you might be changing parsley. An orange Y-shaped gland, called the osmeterium, will emerge from the top of his head. He will also emit a strong sweet smell, which after a while, turns a bit sour. Both the smell and the osmeterium appearance help to ward off predators.

Don't worry. Neither the Eastern Black Swallowtail caterpillar's osmeterium nor the smell are harmful to humans.

Molting

Caterpillars will molt, or shed their skin, up to five times. It is very interesting to watch them shed their skin, but be alert because the molting process is very quick.

The caterpillar pictured here is a fifth instar caterpillar, as he is in his fifth and final skin after molting.

Eastern Black Swallowtail Caterpillar Diagram

Head

True Legs

Thorax

Abdominal Prolegs

Abdomen

Anal Prolegs

Molted Skin

Handling Caterpillars

Don't ever pull a caterpillar from his location, as you may hurt his fragile legs or feet. While the Eastern Black Swallowtail caterpillar is not harmful to humans, I prefer not to handle them because I do not want to inadvertently cause any injury or stress to the caterpillars.

Approaching the End

When the caterpillar is about the size of a human pinky finger, with bright green and black stripes and yellow spots, he is approaching the end of the caterpillar stage. On average, this is when he is about 13 days old. I have found that hotter weather results in a shorter caterpillar stage. Depending on the temperature and the weather, the caterpillar can be near the end as early as 8 days old to as late as 18 days old. If you haven't already done so, add sticks to the nursery, as it is almost time for him to leave the parsley. Arrange clean, leaf-free and pest-free sticks throughout the nursery. Sticks should touch each other but not reach outside of the nursery lid. Otherwise, the caterpillar will escape.

Top Right: Caterpillar 9 days old, fourth instar stage
Middle Right: Caterpillar 12 days old, fifth instar stage
Bottom Right: Caterpillars 8 days old, fourth instar stage on left, and 12 days old, fifth instar stage on right
Bottom Left: Nursery with caterpillars of various ages

16

<u>Roaming</u>: When he nears the end of life as a caterpillar, the first thing a caterpillar will do is empty his belly, called purging. You will notice a puddle of green liquid (about the size of a penny) in the nursery, which is your signal that he is ready to roam in search of the right "place" for him to make his chrysalis. Some caterpillars find their "place" right away, which may be on a stick, the side of the parsley container, or even the side or the top of the nursery. Others take several hours, even two days, to find the right "place." You will be amazed at how quickly the caterpillar can move when he is roaming: the formerly sluggish eating machine will now be wandering around the nursery at an impressive speed.

In September 2005, I took this photo of the first caterpillars I ever had. These are the caterpillars I mentioned in my Introduction on Page 5, and this photo continues to be one of my favorites. While these caterpillars appear to be kissing, they were actually fighting over the last piece of parsley on the stalks. Both of these caterpillars began to roam the day after I took this photo, and both became chrysalises soon after. The following May, both emerged as butterflies, and were the first two butterflies I ever had who overwintered in their chrysalises.

Once the caterpillar finds his "place," he will shrink in size as he secures himself with a silk-like thread, called his "sling," right under his head. He will also secure his tail region, and will be in a J-shape position. The caterpillar will remain in this position usually from 24 to 72 hours. As time progresses, he will relax more into his sling, his color will fade, and his skin will begin to shrivel.

When the caterpillar is almost ready to begin his metamorphosis, he will start slowly moving back and forth near the head portion of his sling. It almost looks as if he is breathing. This can go on for a matter of minutes, or a matter of hours. Don't go too far though, because it only takes three to four minutes for him to change from a caterpillar into a chrysalis.

As the caterpillar begins to change, his skin will slowly peel back from his head to his tail region, and eventually, the skin will drop off. During the metamorphosis, he will wiggle around frantically as he sheds his skin.

On the following 3 pages, watch how the caterpillar turns into a chrysalis. The entire process took four minutes.

9

10

11

12

13

14

15

16

At first, the chrysalis (also called a pupa or a cocoon) will be bright green with yellow markings. Nature has equipped the chrysalis with the ability to camouflage its surroundings, which helps protect it from predators. Typically, if the chrysalis is on or near something green such as a leaf, it will stay green. If it is on something brown such as a stick, the chrysalis will turn brown after about two hours and actually look like part of the stick. It is interesting to see the chrysalis about halfway through its color change, when it is half green and half brown.

During the summer months, it can take anywhere from 6 to 18 days for a butterfly to emerge from the chrysalis. However, if the chrysalis is formed in late summer or early autumn, the butterfly will most likely "overwinter" in the chrysalis and emerge the following spring. For instance, two of my chrysalises were formed in late September, and the butterflies emerged during the last week of the following April.

I've read that some people bring their chrysalises into the house but I would advise against it. If the butterfly emerges during the winter, fresh flower nectar is not readily available and the butterfly cannot survive without it. If you have a chrysalis that overwinters, take precautions to protect your nursery from becoming filled with or surrounded by snow and/or ice. When I have overwintering chrysalises, I keep my nursery in my unheated shed during the winter months. I will return the nursery to its original location outside under a large table after I am sure it will not snow anymore.

Even though it is dormant, a chrysalis is a living creature. Do not disturb the chrysalis for at least 48 hours after it is formed. Always treat the chrysalis with care, no matter how old it is.

Sometimes a butterfly will never emerge from the chrysalis. If a chrysalis turns completely black, or does not emerge after a lengthy time in the summer months, it wasn't meant to be. Remove the chrysalis from the nursery when you are certain that it will not produce a butterfly.

The Eastern Black Swallowtail Butterfly typically emerges in the morning hours because the warm sunlight helps dry his wings, although I have had some that emerged in the afternoon. Before the butterfly emerges, the chrysalis will turn almost transparent, and you will actually be able to see the butterfly through the chrysalis. Overwintering chrysalises, however, do not turn as transparent as those ready to emerge in the summer months.

It only takes about three minutes for a butterfly to completely emerge from the chrysalis. The head end of the chrysalis will crack open, and the butterfly will crawl out of it head first. Immediately after emerging, his wings will be very wrinkled, and he will move his wings back and forth to pump fluid into them. He will then hang upside down for about an hour or two in order to straighten and dry his wings.

Do not handle a newly emerged butterfly for at least an hour, because his wings are very fragile. Also, do not keep your newly emerged butterfly trapped for too long, because soon he will be ready to fly into the world and will need to find nectar to eat.

On the following 2 pages, watch the butterfly emerge from the chrysalis, and note how his wings take form throughout the process.

The emergence of the butterfly is truly amazing. It took approximately 20 minutes to get from Photo 1 to Photo 20. Photo 21 shows the empty chrysalis.

Now the fun begins! This is a great time to take photographs of your new butterfly, as his wings are not yet ready for flight. Gently allow him to crawl onto your hand, and you can place him on flowers for some great photos. Even though he cannot fly just yet, he will like to walk over your fingers, or up and down your arm. The butterfly will beat his wings a bit to help them dry, which is completely natural. Be gentle with your new friend, and never pull him off his location because his legs and wings are very fragile.

The butterfly will fly when the time is right. I enjoy having the butterfly walk around on my fingers one last time, then while I stretch my arm upwards with him on my fingertips, I watch as he takes his first flight into the world.

Eastern Black Swallowtail Butterfly Diagram

Antenna

Fore Wing

Head

Compound Eye

Proboscis

Hind Wing

Thorax

Abdomen

Leg

Eye Spot

The butterfly on the left, with a more defined band of yellow spots, is a male. The butterfly on the right, with more blue towards the end of the hind wings, is a female. Note the butterfly's eye spots, which are a part of the hind wings. The eye spots help scare off potential predators and also play a role in butterfly courtship.

The lifespan of the Eastern Black Swallowtail Butterfly is about two weeks. The butterfly you just released may return and pay you a visit on your flowers or butterfly bush. Perhaps it will lay eggs on your parsley if it is female. Thus continues the butterfly's circle of life.

Congratulations on completing the journey of these delicate tapestries! You successfully raised an Eastern Black Swallowtail Butterfly from egg to flight, and you have added more beauty to our wonderful world. I hope you found the experience to be fun, interesting and rewarding.

Perhaps the delicate tapestry I will remember the most is the one I named "Nemo." He emerged late in the day on August 12, 2006 with a curled right hind wing. Because this wing was curled, he could not fly. I kept him in the nursery overnight so that he would not fall victim to predators. The following morning, Nemo was alive but still could not fly. Fearing he would die from starvation, I quickly made some sugar water, which I put on my hand. I let Nemo crawl around on my hand, and sure enough, he unrolled his proboscis and began drinking the sugar water right from my hand. I put Nemo back into the nursery when he was done eating. I drenched a little sponge with the sugar water and hung it in the nursery, and Nemo found it and drank from it. Later that day, I took him out again, and he flapped his wings very hard as he tried to take flight. After about three minutes, Nemo finally took off and flew away. A short time later, he came back and flew all around me, as if he was saying, "Look! I can do it! Thank you!" Then, Nemo flew away for good, leaving me standing there with a tear in my eye, thankful for such an encounter. The butterfly pictured here is not Nemo, but a delicate tapestry I raised in 2010.

Glossary of Terms

Abdomen: the segmented tail region of both the caterpillar and the butterfly which contains the heart, reproductive organs, and digestive system. Additionally, the caterpillar's abdomen contains 4 pairs of abdominal prolegs.

Antenna: the sensory appendage attached to the butterfly's head, used for the sense of smell and balance. Butterflies have two antennae with clubs at the end.

Chrysalis: the inactive, hard shell in which the butterfly forms, also called a cocoon or pupa

Compound Eye: the convex eye of the butterfly, containing several separate light-sensitive units

Fore Wing: the two upper wings on either side of the butterfly

Frass: caterpillar droppings

Eye Spot: the orange spots near the end of the butterfly's hind wings which look like eyes

Head: The head of the butterfly contains the brain, two eyes, the proboscis and antennae, whereas the head of the caterpillar contains the brain, mandible (jaw), eyes, antennae and osmeterium.

Hind Wing: the two lower wings on either side of the butterfly

Instar: the caterpillar's stage of development between molts. For example, a fifth instar caterpillar has molted for the fifth and last time.

Larva: another term for caterpillar

Leg: Eastern Black Swallowtail Butterflies have six legs, whereas the caterpillars have six true legs (3 pairs), 8 abdominal prolegs (4 pairs) and 1 pair of anal prolegs.

Metamorphosis: changing of form from one life stage to another, i.e. from a caterpillar into a chrysalis

Molt: shedding the skin which is replaced by new growth

Osmeterium: an orange y-shaped gland that emerges from the caterpillar's head. It emits a strong sweet-to-sour smelling scent and is the caterpillar's defense mechanism.

Overwinter: spending the entire winter in the chrysalis form. Some chrysalises formed in late summer/early autumn will not emerge until the following spring.

Place: the location chosen by the caterpillar in preparation for his metamorphosis

Proboscis: a spiral, straw-like tube on the head of the butterfly used to sip nectar

Pupa: another term for chrysalis or cocoon

Purging: when the caterpillar empties his belly before he begins to roam

Roaming: the caterpillar's act of searching for the right "place" to change into a chrysalis

Sling: the silk-like thread made by the caterpillar in which he secures himself before changing into a chrysalis

Thorax: the body section of the caterpillar and butterfly between the head and the abdomen. The butterfly's legs and wings are attached to the thorax, whereas the caterpillar's true legs are attached to the thorax.

Resources

Web Sites

Berkeley's Anise Swallowtail Web Site: http://www.berkeleyswallowtails.com

The Butterfly Conservation Initiative: http://www.butterflyrecovery.org/

The Butterfly Website: http://www.butterflywebsite.com

North America Butterfly Association: http://www.naba.org

Eastern Black Swallowtail Species Information:
http://www.butterfliesandmoths.org/species/Papilio-polyxenes

Fairfax County Public Schools Eastern Black Swallowtail Web Site:
http://www.fcps.edu/islandcreekes/ecology/eastern_black_swallowtail.htm

Books

Butterflies Through Binoculars: The East-A Field Guide to the Butterflies of Eastern North America by Jeffrey Glassberg. Publisher: Oxford University Press, 1999. ISBN-10 # 0195106687

Caterpillars in the Field and Garden: A Field Guide to the Butterfly Caterpillars of North America by Thomas J. Allen, James P. Brock and Jeffrey Glassberg. Publisher: Oxford University Press, 2005. ISBN-10 # 0195149874

A Field Guide to Eastern Butterflies by Paul A. Opler (author), Vichai Malikus (illustrator) and Roger Tory Peterson (series editor). Publisher: Houghton Mifflin, 1998. ISBN-10 # 0395904536

A Field Guide to Western Butterflies by Paul A. Opler (author), Amy Bartlett Wright (illustrator) and Roger Tory Peterson (series editor). Publisher: Houghton Mifflin, 1999. ISBN-10 # 0395791529

Florida's Fabulous Butterflies by Thomas C. Emmel (author) and Brian Kenney (editor). Publisher: World Publications, 1997. ISBN-10 # 0911977155

The Life Cycles of Butterflies: From Egg to Maturity, a Visual Guide to 23 Common Garden Butterflies by Judy Burris and Wayne Richards. Publisher: Storey Publishing LLC, 2006. ISBN-10 # 1580176178

National Audubon Society Field Guide to North American Butterflies. Publisher: Alfred A. Knopf; Chanticleer Press, 1981. ISBN-10 # 0394519140

National Wildlife Federation Attracting Birds, Butterflies & Backyard Wildlife by David Mizejewski. Publisher: Creative Homeowner, 2004. ISBN-10 # 1580111505

Peterson First Guide to Caterpillars of North America by Amy Bartlett Wright (author) and Roger Tory Peterson (series editor). Publisher: Houghton Mifflin, 1998. ISBN-10 # 0395911842

The Secret Lives of Backyard Bugs: Discover Amazing Butterflies, Moths, Spiders, Dragonflies, and Other Insects! by Judy Burris and Wayne Richards. Publisher: Storey Publishing LLC, 2011. ISBN-10 # 1603429859

"May the wings of the butterfly kiss the sun
And find your shoulder to light on,
To bring you luck, happiness and riches
Today, tomorrow and beyond."
- Irish Blessing

About the Author:

Jill Marie Ocone is an award-winning photographer and high school English and journalism teacher. She has a bachelor's degree in English from Rutgers University and a master's degree in Curriculum, Instruction and Technology from Nova Southeastern University. Jill is a member of Professional Photographers of America, Wedding & Portrait Photographers International, Society of Event & Sports Photographers, and many local art guilds. A lifelong resident of Point Pleasant, New Jersey, Jill enjoys creating visual memories with her camera, learning about our world's interesting creatures, and vacationing at Florida's Space and Treasure Coasts. Visit Jill at www.photocone.com.